A CAMERA OBSCURA

A CAMERA OBSCURA

poems

Carl Marcum

Red Hen Press | *Pasadena, CA*

A Camera Obscura

Book design by Mark E. Cull

Library of Congress Cataloging-in-Publication Data

Names: Marcum, Carl, author.
Title: A camera obscura : poems / Carl Marcum.
Description: First Edition. | Pasadena, CA : Red Hen Press, [2021]
Identifiers: LCCN 2020056368 (print) | LCCN 2020056369 (ebook) | ISBN 9781597094818 (trade paperback) | ISBN 9781597091190 (epub)
Subjects: LCGFT: Poetry.
Classification: LCC PS3563.A63665 C36 2021 (print) | LCC PS3563.A63665 (ebook) | DDC 811/.54—dc23
LC record available at https://lccn.loc.gov/2020056368
LC ebook record available at https://lccn.loc.gov/2020056369

Publication of this book has been made possible in part through the financial support of Jim Wilson.

The National Endowment for the Arts, the Los Angeles County Arts Commission, the Ahmanson Foundation, the Dwight Stuart Youth Fund, the Max Factor Family Foundation, the Pasadena Tournament of Roses Foundation, the Pasadena Arts & Culture Commission and the City of Pasadena Cultural Affairs Division, the City of Los Angeles Department of Cultural Affairs, the Audrey & Sydney Irmas Charitable Foundation, the Kinder Morgan Foundation, the Meta & George Rosenberg Foundation, the Albert and Elaine Borchard Foundation, the Adams Family Foundation, the Riordan Foundation, Amazon Literary Partnership, the Sam Francis Foundation, and the Mara W. Breech Foundation partially support Red Hen Press.

First Edition
Published by Red Hen Press
www.redhen.org

MIX
Paper from responsible sources
FSC® C011935

Acknowledgments

Grateful acknowledgment is given to the editors of the publications and journals in which some of these poems first appeared, sometimes in different versions:

Arizona Highways, "Blind Contour: Night Sky № 1"; *jmww150*, "Cuaresma," "The Romantic Mode Overheard," "Dispatch"; *Kenyon Review Blog*, "Final Epistle to My Grad School Self,"; *Latinx Rising: An Anthology of Latinx Science Fiction and Fantasy*, "A Science Fiction," "Sci-Fi Ku"; *Luna Luna Magazine*, "Further Notes from The Art Institute"; *Pleiades*, "[Dark Matter]"; *Poetry East*, "Word Assimilation," "Field Notes w/ Stripped Trailer," "Last Law of Memento"; *Puro Chicanx Writers of the 21st Century*, "Poem Missing My Mother," "Un Miércoles en Febero"; and *The Wind Shifts: New Latino Poets* "Barrio Brisbane Bears Witness," "First Snow," "Notes from the Art Institute."

I am very grateful for the generous support of the following programs and institutions that provided space, time, forum, and finances to make this book possible: the Wallace Stegner Fellowship at Stanford University; the National Endowment for the Arts; the Illinois Arts Council; the D. H. Lawrence Fellowship at the Taos Writers' Conference and the University of New Mexico; the Ragdale Foundation; the National Aeronautics and Space Administration; the Guild Complex; Letras Latinas; Canto Mundo; and DePaul University.

Special and particular thanks for invaluable support, friendship, consejo y ejemplo to Richard Jones, Bayo Olayinka Ojikutu, Alison Deming, Lorna Dee Cervantes, Luis Alberto Urrea, Carmen Giménez Smith, Vincent Cioffi, Kevin Gonzalez, Laurie Ann Guerrero, Luivette Resto, Diana Marie Delgado, Urayoán Noel, Brian Tierney, Caroline Goodwin, Francisco Aragón, Erin Teegarden, Ellen Placey Wadey, Dan Stolar, Eric Selinger, W. S. Di Piero, Ken Fields, August Kleinzahler, Neil Chudgar, Tom Collins, Sarah Graef, Josh Brown, Mike Larkin, Norma Elia Cantú, María Meléndez, David Welch, Rosebud Ben-Oni, Eduardo C. Corral, Terrance Hayes, and the Late-Greats: Eavan Boland, Steve Orlen, Jon Anderson, and Tony Hoagland.

A special thanks to my former students. You guys inspired me too.

Unending gratitude to Evangelina Marcum, John and Patti LaVelle, Nicole Leventhal and the Vic and Diane Leventhal guest quarters, the Foleys, and most especially, to M. Stephanie Murray, and Clark Felix, and Maeve Maria Inez, my guides, my stars, my destinations.

In Memory of USAF Senior Master Sergeant, Carl Lee Marcum, 1948–2020

Contents

Introduction 11

Cartografía de Noche 15

☀

Blind Contours: Night Sky № 1 19
Blind Contours: Night Sky № 2 21
Displacement 22
Triangulation 23
Brokedown Elegy with a Ghost Inside It 25
Field Notes w/ Stripped Trailer 27
Immolation: Landscape 29
Chicago: Ruthless 30
Elemental 31
Etymology of Cute 32
Notes from the Art Institute 34
Further Notes from the Art Institute 36
Bad Wolf 38
Purgatory Adjacent: A Dreamscape 39
Twenty-Three Weeks 40
Autumn, Chicago 41
First Snow 43
Woolgathering 45
Word Assimilation 48
Castigo 50
A Science Fiction 51

⁕ ⁕

The Hubble Meditations

i. Messier Object 31 55

ii. Horsehead Nebula 57

iii. Ojo de Dios 60

iv. η Carinae 61

v. Pillars of Creation 63

vi. Ultra Deep Field Image 64

⁕ ⁕ ⁕

[Dark Matter] 67

Blind Contours: Night Sky № 3 69

Blind Contours: Night Sky № 4 70

SciFi-ku 71

Dispatch 74

Grief at the Movies Scrawled in the Dark 76

Second Dispatch 77

Thirty-Six Weeks 78

Untitled with Teeth Brushed 79

Poem Missing My Mother 80

My Father, Headed East 81

Self-Portrait, Hand Tinted 82

Cuaresma

Restos Mortales 83

Viernes Santo 84

Pascua 85

Passion Play 86

Un Miércoles en Febrero 89

Middle March 90

Guesswork Ending in a Levis Fragment 91

Interruption in *One Hundred Years of Solitude* 92

Barrio Brisbane Bears Witness 94

The Nostalgic Mode 97

The Romantic Mode Overheard 98

Manny's Luck Runs Out: A Parlor Trick 99

Final Epistle to My Grad-School Self 102

$\boldsymbol{N} = \boldsymbol{R}^{*} \text{ x } f_p \text{ x } \boldsymbol{n}_e \text{ x } f_\ell \text{ x } f_i \text{ x } f_c \text{ x } \boldsymbol{L}$ **:** " $\forall$ " 103

Fulano's Last Law of Memento 105

Notes 107

Introduction

Roland Barthes makes a distinction about the way photography registers for the viewer, and the most apt term for defining the vision of Carl Marcum's *A Camera Obscura* is "punctum," the prick of recognition and emotional tenor a photo has on its beholder. How does looking change the viewer? In the case of Marcum's wide-ranging and ambitious second collection, the poet releases himself from what he knows of his gaze to uncover not-knowing as access to private and public sublimity.

Marcum's collection lives in the heaven of faith and the heaven of stars set against the landscape of the Southwest and the new contexts of his adulthood: Chicago, fatherhood, the quotidian life of desks, *Star Trek*, and the progress of a pregnancy in poems that chart "birth's violent certainty."

The feel of punctum is also enacted through Marcum's shrewd vision, which recalls Coleridge's expansive and vulnerable view of the universe. In "First Snow," Marcum speaks to his mother's nostalgia for Arizona as they hold each other in Utah's frosty winter outside.

> I had you
> to myself again.
> We stood against
> the cold and foreign
> light of a Utah
> winter window;
> the snow falling
> hours on end
> and my childhood
> delight with the
> constant flurry.
> Our faces reflected
> in spider-frosted

panes, and I could
see you fill with
sorrow as each
astonishing
flake tilted through
our view.

One of the book's great beauties is Marcum's ability to see again what is inside the emotional landscape of others, particularly his mother, who is a potent subject in the book. This book of celestial inscription also considers Marcum's conflicted Chicano identity through the lens of his Catholicism in the poem "Un Miércoles en Febrero," in which a child inquires about the ash on his forehead and his response might sum up the book's central question:

Faith is doubt,
hijo mio, remember this: we are dust, we are
stars—we are what happened and what is next.

A book that can look in the heavens and also into the interior so ably speaks to me as a reader, the punctum one feels, what Barthes describes as "that accident which pricks me (but also bruises me, is poignant to me)." The accident is the vulnerability and acute lens Marcum brings to this cohesive and sweeping collection.

—Carmen Giménez Smith

A CAMERA OBSCURA

Cartografía de Noche

Aquí

está

la luna, nueva

y llena

a la

misma vez.

Y

de este momento,

siguen otros momentos—

y

si sigues

las luces

plateadas,

puede ser

que llegarás

aquí.

It's a strange courage
you give me ancient star.

—William Carlos Williams

Blind Contours: Night Sky

|*| № 1

Tonight, the heavens murmur their promise:
bright and distant violence. And you've driven
a switchback road out past jagged, small
mountains that border west this small and jagged
town where your heart's consecutive failures

have been as carefully charted as the codex
of stars folded *in-out—in-out* and tucked away
in your breast pocket. Because tonight you hate
yourself for being lonely, recline against
hood and windshield, dark and parked

and gazing—because this is all you know.
Because you misbelieve, because you mistake
yourself for ancient: vision unveiled by saguaros
yearning skyward—arms beckoning the gauzy
ribbon of dust and stars as the stun and halo

of headlights fade from your eyes' edges;
though you're still left dark and wandering.
Apogee begins to focus: Betelgeuse, Rigel
arm and leg of Orion—his belt, those
diamond seams . . . and you forget

why it is he stalks the skies. Draw your eyes
back. See the night for all her breadth
when coyotes ring the pale and petty

arguments. And catch now, peripherally,
a streaking light, an acute and failing

angle earthward—all atmosphere and friction,
a brilliant production. A meteor, you know,
milliseconds away from smoldering *-ite.*
And because it may amount to nothing—
a quintessence of dust—cast that well-worn wish.

|* *| № 2

A clot of cloud cover, low and heavy
with snow not ready yet to fall. February

twilight, a south by southwest tumbling
in this axis toward dark fixes the clouds

a slightly terrible pink—red shift. The wind
drives hard toward the lake, pulling condensed

selves into gaps, into absolute blue vertigo
—gravity turning mass: a spiraling so

deft, so daft it holds the bare trees as night
fills the distance amongst the network

of longing, amongst the branching ache.
The sky's all mottled, a confused room:

coral and cobalt. And the whole city under
the impression we're each inhabited

by love's blue-eyed boy. The evening
star pulls us into bearing, into the arc

that keeps us steady, though her son's
determined to cloud our eyes, though

Venus is a mirror of atmosphere, though
she is constant, though we mistake her for star.

Displacement

Starlight's the only cast, the stalwart earth
against our spines—aligned amidst the heavens.
Lest we not forget, *to displace* is to supplant
by geometrical relation between the initial position
of a body and the dark whorls of the mind unspooling
in the night. The meander of Andromeda tilts
the horizon; we are where we never expected.

An eye and its motion: continuous sequencing,
indexing, suffusing toward witness. That is to say,
the fortunes read in wide and turning skies, what we
make believe to be, the ground beneath us—gravity's
unshakeable faith in falling which pulls our instinct
to the stars, those lights that slowly spin us reckless.

Triangulation

37.77° N, 122.41° W

Adjust my heart for declination, once
toward each bridge that abandons the city.
Now, divide the horizon between us by half, then
half again—the moon, that broken
stone cast through your window, mine,
those ancient phone bills, extensive.

⁕

32.22° N, 110.92° W

Our glimmer in the cracked windshield
winding down Euclid Avenue, that street
that begged and begged at night for
fifth gear. I hold you like this: cackling;
errant; strand of hair caught in the corner
of your mouth, something I said, funny.

⁕

41.87° N, 87.62° W

We'll find each other by uttered accident
in the flower shop down the street.
So I'll talk you out of asters, and you'll talk
me out of tulips, and instead we'll walk
home laughing and coincidental.
Or I'll find you this way: your hands

full of trinkets and Sunday, breeze tousling
off the lake—*Look!* you'll smile,
Glow-in-the-dark cats! Can I get 'em?

Brokedown Elegy with a Ghost Inside It

My Darling pegs a kiss to her hand, then the roof
of the van whenever we pass hazard lights, raised
hoods, the defunct, marooned, and otherwise stranded.

I-80 corridor makes way to hog and corn, Nebraska's
flat redundancy—Platte River, five, six times.
Continental Divide, Wyoming rain and eggs underdone.

In Utah, my gut drops out an unexpected ditch.
Salt Lake, I am disconsolate in this café. A maple,
full-June green, stands at the corner of 9 & 9, and Larry,

you've left that pink smudge on the horizon. I won't forgive
your addictions today, though I think you'd be pleased
that Hawaiian shirts are all the season's rage and the sun

still sets where it's become accustomed. Behind me
somewhere a blackening thumbnail teaches a lesson
in patience, a lesson I'm bound to deny, even as that

nail sloughs off, though not for weeks now. And because
I'm a wreck waiting for metal, my Darling guides us past
the sun flaring solstice, past the arid, past rows and rows

of California agriculture where something of Larry still swamps
peaches—peaches I'll buy in a month for my Darling's
cobbler that won't thicken, though I'll eat it à la mode

while my thumb throbs like a phantom. I've never seen ghosts
though I hear them scratching in roves of their slack mouths.
Larry, the mundane measure of your habitual heart failed us; even now,

I wander too far across the center divide, my Darling asleep
against glass. It's your fault, Larry, these oncoming rigs,
blood blooming under that black nail, these miles left to me.

Field Notes w/ Stripped Trailer

Not burned, not fire, but fire's recourse—
	its appetite. The 2x4 & 4x4 frame
discernible as a skeleton. An American-
	built trailer, good sized, double wide,
out away from city lights. The sun moves
	toward a low, pink throb . . .

Isn't this how we've defined our rise
	to knowing man? By what's missing from
our structure, by what's missing from this
	structure? Shadow twist & twilight
begin to color the frame more completely
	abandoned. This ruin kept secrets . . .

Inside is nothing, is bare board & dead wire,
	porcelain artifacts of indoor plumbing:
commode & kitchen sink. Desert
	grasses grow through what's left of peeling
linoleum, beer can & plastic bag & wait,
	inside: a flap of wing, of real, live crow

scavenging these bones for some shining usefulness.
	Wheels gone, siding, walls—everything that
was "home" misinterpreted as "mobile."
	Hope for some deliberate scratch, some
less-than-ancient graffiti to shed light on
	previous inhabitants: TF♥DT, *Pancho was here*,

a crude-painted Walmart—jagged spears, parking lot,
	something of the modern hunt & gather—
anything to connect us to *homo-mobilehomus,*

homo-apartementus, homo-surburbamente.
But because red blood is only tangential,
some percentage of birth & gravity intended

to end abandonment, let fire fill the ruined.
It's easy enough, it's a book of matches:
primeval brace against the dark,
smolder & spark.

Immolation: Landscape

Not a stand of trees, just two. Should they look
like men in this half-light? This bleary eye?
One on each river bank, leafless nerve bundles
conducting a history between them—heavy with silt,
cult and progress. Each bend, a curve of decay:
the concentric hoods of each tributary
adding its mulled wine, its broken dish.
Should the right name be written in the winding
sediment, this hand will blaze—canopies brittle
as this creased photo march toward ash.
This method of destruction has proven
more equitable. Confess: the horizon between us
is charred at the edges, swollen.

Chicago: Ruthless

Nothing seems certain
as the particulars of train
rush over Adams Street.
                    This spectacle
does not pertain to me: not
the petunias in bloom, not
the coffee, or my own acidic stomach.
                    Soy tanta cuidad—lost in the vertical:
industrious towers, metered, parallel cars,
double-parked deliveries flashing
those yellow excuses. Clark Street,
La Salle bus. Pitch of sirens
and blisters on my feet from mile
after flagrant mile of big shoulder
concrete.
          The intermittent sun.
What's mine: this temporary sense
of grid-marked east and west, novelty of glass,
jittery zigzag of fire escape. Page
after page: classified opportunity and shade.
                    Pedestrian crush, crosswalk,
rattling rails: stoppage of thought—bulb-flash,
filament-pop. A pigeon, a partition,
day-old doughnuts and the train
          —ruthless   ruthless—
schedules to break to the end of the line.

Elemental

Storm front all rained out.
The wind though, a persistent grudge
tearing away hats, pulling ribs

from umbrellas. It's comical
how I'm trudging up Aldine
like something silent,

slow motives, without breath.
And leaves start to spiral
into an orange-brown helix I recognize

as dangerous, but my body's
too thick to move aside
and autumn swirls about me,

lifts me flash-strobed,
from the common sidewalk—cyclonic—
and I can do nothing but burst

out laughing till I'm set lightly
down, black boots, concrete, gravity's
dull embrace. Everything

that was movement:
now sudden, now still, no hint
of my baptism by air.

Etymology of Cute

Cute, from acute
from the Latin *acuere*
to sharpen to a point,
an angle, as in exhibit A:
the perfect nose, which
is cute, as in small
and well-formed, but
not so small as to
seem peculiar, but rather
to be cute, and in such
a to give a face
an appropriate
idiom.

A cute face establishes
attractiveness, that is to say
rounded, and young,
clearly complected
so as to inspire
the desire to mate.
Cute, from the Old English
cunnan, Which is cunning,
which is to know in a learned
way. Which is cute in itself.
That is to say, to know
you are cute. *Mignon*,
in French, as in kissing;
as in what the cute face
elicits from the mouth.

And from the French,
mignon, minion—
favored, and mannered,
a lover who is insincere.
Too cute, which is keen,
which is sharp and to
the point, like the daggers
elicited from the mouth.
Cute as in sharp-witted,
which is perceptive.
Which is to say, don't
get cute with me.

Notes from the Art Institute

Zapata, José Clemente Orozco, oil on canvas, 1930

If I'd grown from the same branch
as Juanito back on Bantam Drive:

I'm fucking serious, whiteboy.

I'd like to think that *that*
is what I'd say seconds
before singing a switchblade
into existence:

I'm fucking serious.
Whiteboy.
Knife.

But as it is, I'm not bothered in this crowd . . .
Their backs turned to me, mine to them.
Hopper's *Nighthawks* draws their famous
attention, not this minor Mexican muralist . . .

. . . And Zapata looms massive in the doorway,
red, brown, white and silhouette. Knife
and his eye, a broken moon. And the foreground
cowers beneath him.

Fucking serious.

Zapata, that brown boot
in your doorway.

Knife.

His eyes, somber under his sombrero's shade, the flat
gaze of gesso. His hands, obscured—am I to assume
his knife? Assume my fist in the cold flash
of mettle—honed edge of have to:

Whiteboy.

Give me wide berth through to the pre-Columbian exhibit.
I know the Toltecs, the Aztecs, the Mayans
believed in human rites and the blades that enforce them

Further Notes from the Art Institute

Xipe Totec, The Flayed One,
Ritual Figurine, Carved Wood & Human Skin, ca. 1450

Tonight, dear one,
by the waning moon
I will take this jet shard,
keen with mercy, along
the seam of your
rigorous spine
and flay a proficient
suit of you
for my finery.

Dear one, your raw
and fecund sinew
assures my bounty:
another harvest,
another generation
of hands emptied,
hanging like bracelets
from my arms.

Your handsome
face a better countenance
from my high cheeks.
I see through the slats
of your eyes. I speak
incantation and renewal
—my tongue
aligned along
your lips. Do not

mourn your blued
and sanguine life
elapsing along the groove
of this blade.

What is driven
through the veins
turns crimson, adorns
the living with promise:
sacrifice preserves
order in the universe.
I will wear your skin,
dear one, among your own
people. They will always
mistake me for kind.

Bad Wolf

I know the moral & what moves me.
This untidy habit of the mouth—the wish
of teeth & tongue to fasten & sate the
longing in the belly—pulls of flesh:
thus the struggling throat of some pretty,
puny thing between predetermined jaws.
These matted hues, dark fleece, this clever wolf
underneath. I know this will be the undoing.
The tinge of tendon, sink of muscle. Teeth
made for unmaking. No huffing, nor puffing.
No grandma-ma's gristle. Only dark woods
& teeth. Only the daft & red & riding of this grim
& certain truth: A wolf is a wolf, & that is the door.

Purgatory Adjacent: A Dreamscape

The office is windowless, the desks in tandem.
You remember your office mate, but haven't seen
him in an age. The walls are beige. There is 1 phone
that seldom rings, & when it sings, your answer is
static tones & rolling bones—fax tolling dazed connection.
1 computer blinks & the uplink loads dial-up slow.
What is waiting after all, but a suffering of fools? The desk
bare-boned: stapler, inbox, 1 failing pen—the mouse
tethered to a fraying cord & cursor-coordinates flux
loose as teeth. The desktop files are each & all empty
sacks that correspond with some sin you cannot recall
omitting. What was reality but representation? You've written
something—*el espejo me espera*. Time collapses into blank
& buzzing light. Something is bound to happen.

Twenty-Three Weeks

Autumn settles with a hot bath;
the moon, a spilled spot scarcely full.

Already Orion filters over the lake
—the harvest of a hunkering down.
Water rushes into the claw-foot tub.
All summer the young sparrowhawk
grew braver. From the veranda last
afternoon, he buckled from the telephone
wire—plunged past my sight behind
garages lining the alley—rose again,
a matted mouse in his talons. The natural

order indifferent as the city. The faucet
steams, the bath arranged as the
certainty of a winter child slides
into the water with you, buoyant.

Autumn, Chicago

What are you listening for? The slow
march to sleep, chimes
in the empty branches, the patterns
leaves keep? Or the scrape
of the scattered scuttle
—a small boat north of harbor;
bow, aft deck, flotsam? The captain survived.
He is still cursing. Tonight's rain will leave
stubborn clouds and the lake gray as geese.

✳

Autumn slips through your window
like an inappropriate girl who
leaves your covers cold, your throat sore.
She has a smile like a dress, flushed cheeks,
dry lips, her russet nail polish all chipped.
A bad girl in a bad-girl coat, she winks
her doe eyes, steals your shirt, kicks off
her panties in the street. She's waiting
for a bus. She waits and smokes.
She sings along with a country song: cheap,
cheap and train whistle, long,
long and copse of thistle. Lost her cat,
lost her keys, lost her panties in the street.
She asks your document, a daisy;
your notary, a pink-white aster, a mottled
rose pressed between her illicit paragraphs.

⁂

You lack ambition in the limited
kitchen where the radiator mutters
and sighs. Coffee keeps the hour late,
bitter in spite of sugar, in spite
of the dissolved. Solution means
suspended: rain clings heavy along telephone
wires—strung pre-Christmas nights,
those little catches of light, dumb
to gravity, to their last brilliant
addition to the almanac. Belly growls
a craving you can't taste. Far off
windows enchant: silhouette, silhouette,
almost-a-face at this distance. Empty
squares of *work-early* or *out-late*
tell their third floor story of exhaust
stack steam, boiler room dreams, plumes
yellowing in city light. Moonrise is
a half-empty glass. Autumn, you are
a pessimist and it's past your bedtime.

First Snow

November's commotion
settles
on my shoulders
like good fortune.
I'm still
delighted
by the white idea
that's begun
to fill the city:
accumulation
and decree
—specific
under my boot.
Remember us,
Mother? You,
postpartum, sister
asleep in another room.
I had you
to myself again.
We stood against
the cold and foreign
light of a Utah
winter window;
the snow falling
hours on end
and my childhood
delight with the
constant flurry.
Our faces reflected
in spider-frosted
panes, and I could

see you fill with
sorrow as each
astonishing
flake tilted through
our view. I know now,
as the city
forgets itself
in the chaos
and grace of ice,
how you yearned south
—missing the desert
the way I watch
out this window
missing you
with each
gathering star.

Woolgathering

Wear gray wool suit and overcoat.
Pack olive sweater; burgundy sweater.
How you managed to know to dress
for snow with your desert blood
escapes you:

But remember:
riding the streets of Nogales with your prima,
Marcella. An afternoon early and hot before
a carne asada, on errand for ice and rolling up
the widows—you had to sweat to look cool
past the group of vatos standing the street
corner. Their tank-top machismo rippling off
them in waves of late summer sun. You were
sixteen maybe, gangly for your age. Haircut
and glasses made you look so obviously gringo.

Car coat, knit cap, scarf, gloves—
insulated against the snow's
sudden dance of apostrophes.
"¿Como es que llegé aqui,
tan legós de le tierra donde nací?"

So, Marcella says
"Wear this," hands you her dad's cap, the one
he kept on the seat but never wore, *Coors* scrolled
across the crown and red as the vato's do-rag slouching
low against his brow the way he slouches on the corner.

Sunglasses betray your
desert residency, while you

wait through bright twenty
degrees for the next bus south.

Marcella hands you a pair
of sunglasses sitting on the dash, you scramble to follow
instruction—hot black plastic across your nose, the hat,
too big and riding down past the tips of your ears.
"Now put your arm around me," Marcella says, nods
over to the vatos on the corner, "Ricky," she says,
"we're gonna make him jealous." And you start to motor by.

Tug the knit cap down past
your ears—you were told
but didn't know how cold
the wind would oppress.
Gabriel says "You look
like a cholo freezing his ass off."
"Órale," you shiver.

The car a sudden oven convecting sun past rolled up
windows. Marcella smiles out, bandana-boy smiles back
—faces suspended in the heat of glass, curvature and turn.

Your face lit from
the inside of the El
window, racketing
through underground
stations. "There I am
again," vanity smiles.
Another you and another

window: each self-division,
dividing endlessly—all remainders—

"Riding low, going slow."
Marcella nudges you and cranks her window down. Air chilling
against moist arms and faces. "The ice is melting fast," you say,
"Why'd we roll up the windows anyway?" She laughs.
"So he'd think we have air conditioning!"

Word Assimilation

Say with me now, burro. And say with me now, buey.
Ass and ox, beasts that bear your burden.

Now whisper this—hermosa, beautiful, she's beautiful.
That's her there, wandering quietly through rooms,
a cart of housekeeping at each door. She empties
my ashtray, makes up my bed, hangs fresh towels.

Now say with me, esposo. Husband. Hers. She smiles
with him in the basement as he pulls used cotton from
her cart, feeds it by the armload to industrial wash and detergent.
Sonrisa, smile—theirs—one on each tired face, these quiet
intersections of labor before lunch.

Juntos, together, them on a sunny bench behind the Mirage
Hotel. Comiendo, thin ham—jamón, jamón rye,
boiled egg, papitas, cold soda from the fourth-floor machine
where it's mysteriously a quarter cheaper. Viviendo en el
momento, por el momento. In the moment—for the moment.
It's not hard to romanticize them—their hands, their hearts.
Not hard. But more than that,
it's wrong.
Wrong to belittle their courage for the third,
fourth time packed in a van with sweat and worry, seventeen
people, a 4:00 a.m. crossing when the moon's gone cold.

Esta vez. Esta vez sí vamos a llegar, sí vamos a empezar,
sí vamos a escapar la vida inútil. And by van, and by bus,
by truckbed, by train and by foot. All the way to the plain,
high-neon chaparral.

Now say, hermano—brother.
His brother with the foothold, foot-in-the-door, door held open,
puerta abierta. Abrazo, embrace, theirs—the brothers.
Bienvenidos. Trabajo. Mañana, tan pronto, y para los dos.

If you're looking for truth here, it's only in passing.
If you're looking for her, she's in a room dreaming.
If you're looking for them, imagine no English.
If you're looking for work, see me at the door.

Castigo

The gray cell of coastal winter
begins to relent at the edges.
Daffodils droop their yellow heads
to rain, to gaze, to periodic sun.

I've muttered my way through another
foreign season, whittled ancient
driftwood—turning its length again
and again in my hands, till it begins

to take on resemblance—
—a door, a dagger, an intern heart:
finally the hinge on which these
sullen hands anticipate return.

Magnolias, five days white, falter them-
selves against the uncivil shore breeze:
their ballast bridal-dance. Hinge, pared
down to a key. *Useless, useless . . .*

I will serve this sentence and slip
into next season's parole, unreformed.
Gather in my arms a bundle
of camellias mistaken for roses.

A Science Fiction

When the sun rose it was smaller
than in my dream. I had been asleep
for what felt a long time, and woke
confused and claustrophobic.
The texture of sky still magnetized me,
a desert bright day. But the light is streaked
like too much everything pulled to the edges
of a window in storm. What little of me exists
as aperture. I wanted so little for my birthday,
a moment's peace on a hill. And where
did that get me? Into the stars themselves?
To hitch myself to a salvage run,
thirteen years round trip? A distress signal,
a freighter the company had written off
the summer I learned to kiss a girl until she
shook with desire, when the engines
fired no one thought to think,
could even know this uncharted
singularity. At night on Earth I am all of Orion,
at night on Earth I fell tangential into a puddle
of cold rain and rippled the muddied reflection of light
—blurred the confusion of New Chicago
into circuit and solder. This is what I can expect:
gravity, density, volume dissipating. I am
all at once. I studied all night for an exam
I wouldn't pass, slept through a snowfall
that piled itself upon itself. Death isn't the door
you would expect—isn't a carriage kindly
stopping. I celebrated my birthday on a
science rig surveying a binary system.
The galley scrounged up a cake and candle;

I wished myself into consciousness. Proximity alarms should be blaring, but sound is stretched to color, color stitched to light, light solidifying to absence, absent the sequence.

Seeing begins in the dark.

—Li-Young Lee

The Hubble Meditations

i. Messier Object 31

The first instance of otherness
so vast it stays captured in the mesh
of silver-nitrate negative, turned sepia
fingerprint: the whorl of Andromeda.

Compatriot galaxy tuned with stars, thick
and spiraled mirror to our unknown. First
noted as *Little Cloud* in Al-Sufi's *Book*
of Fixed Stars, her glow like a candle

through a keyhole as it refracts against
the girdle of her namesake constellation.
Like the myth, her beauty is troublesome
and vacant, chained to a black rock

that shocks the crescent, ambient nude
in Doré's luminous rendition—her
exposure to our monstrous, magnified
eyes. For a thousand generations

she resisted our ken and wrought our
attention, steady, undecipherable beacon.
Edwin Hubble surveyed her in the dark
nights of 1923, a red shorthand in the

corner: *VAR!* denotes her variable
brightness—the measurement of
extragalactic light, that triumph
of exclamation. At last, the beyond

evident as the plumbing of our own
hearts. Paradigms shift, space expands
more mythic than our capacity to comprehend.
Andromeda: named, numbered, catalogued.

ii. Horsehead Nebula

> *A horse is a thing of such beauty . . . none will tire*
> *of looking at him so long as he displays himself*
> *in all his splendor.*
> *—Xenophon*

Imprinted like a glyph in our minds, a pattern born in trance,
        the dream of momentum

rendered against the sensory void
        of darkness—pulled into the earthen-cold

caves of Lascaux and Chauvet where shamans ochered
        animal visions against stone walls.

Imagine the erratum of pre-history:

        a carved ivory tusk
                worn smooth with worry,
                        the Voglehead horse held close
                                as the tribal spears stalk a herd
        of dun ponies to spook,
                        stampede toward the hungry
                                luck of gravity and cliff.

Imagine the first dim soul sensing the absence
                of a horse's back begging
                        for his form.

The scamper astride
an unwitting beast.

The terror and shock,
a ruined stalk:

frenzy breaks
full-gallop across the steppes.

That moment: horse and rider:
tangle of hair and hide
thigh and quarter clench
seismic-blurred landscape
thunder and dust
eccrine perfume
lather and panic—
—in that exchange

two species entwine
irrecoverably,

a new knot
in the strings
of theory

—and rider is thrown
a day's walk away
into a new lack
he cannot fill.

In the old story, the king's son turns the white-starred
        head of an unbroken beast toward the sun,
soothes him with whispers, elides his shadow.

This familiar silhouette, this dearest coincidence,
        so distilled through mirrors and software
that these strange physics cannot help their own

resemblance. Astral red fire, the backdrop of cosmos, each star
        a neuron firing *horse*—queen's knight
in gambit, black steed, Bucephalas bound toward eternity.

iii. Ojo de Dios

Simple to understand: a star like our own that's shed
its outer layers in violent discharge: matter exaggerating

to iris, excited atoms and interstellar medium—a blue
gestalt. It is sky, pond, the sunset of mirrors. It is jay

wing, an oyster shell's pearled past. What is resemblance
but equation? What it is to see: eye to cold technological

eye—spectacle of light translated to electric impulse:
soma to axon, depolarizing and accelerating along myelin,

traverses the optic chiasm, registers primal in the thalamus.
This gasp in luminiferous aether, fluent in the idiom of blue.

Huicholi fathers weave a totem for each child—a Sikuli, a flattened
helix—to imbue sight to unseen, unite the mind with the unknown.

Whose gaze is this? Whose soul growing exponential in darkness?

iv. η Carinae

A million times more light
in her fits of wrath—what each
of us holds in or lets fly
across a room. Blown

as an April tulip along
the lakeshore, past the limit
of conventional beauty
—two teetering petals

hold stubborn to stem,
utterly bicarinated.
She is the inner conflict
writ massive: la lucha, la lucha:

Is she Jacob or Angel?
Is it gravity or radiation that hopes
to keep us each entire?
We begin in division,

cell into cell into cell,
the warring, systemic
mass of us staggering
persistent and exiled

in our own blunt senses.
If light is to sound,
she is dense thunder
and blasted window

—tyrannous discord—
sustain and decay, a rabble
of broken-glassed patina.

v. Pillars of Creation

The patterns of becoming
encoded in interstellar gas—our echo
of destruction, time-lapse
and aftermath. Pillars of star-birth
fused to slow hand
and spire of Monument Valley—those cleaved,
precarious strata rising from the
dust of siltstone
oxidized.
The sunset-streaked furious beyond.
        Or, these pillars
are the silver-nitrate preservation, charred vestige of conflagration:
the jagged cinders of Chicago's
stone and construct
        when chaos
consumed all that would feed and flash
        the fire's dervish.
Understanding is rote superimposition—images
stacked like books in the mess,
each edge of embrace, each mistake.

vi. Ultra Deep Field Image

More than the mind can parse,
this pinpoint of sky magnified
to mosaic past the vanishing point,
an artisan tile, a cosmic backsplash.

The almost-smatter of tidal pool, or
moonlight against old glass—pitted,
slow as honey gathered, a needle's
eye of night warbled with light

collected, embroidered in black
satin vestments, the children of Nyx:
each spiral, each helix, each beacon
of apparent magnitude. Simulacra

is the persistent mistake, the necessity
of the mind's eye. How else to arrest
this expanse? How else to say this
is simply an image, a small window

dithered between hunter and furnace?
Compiled nights, a revelation, a mirror,
an exposure gathered again and again
—depth of the universe in visible light.

How does this field escape its naming?
Solely itself, the finale of seem.

Force is force, matter is matter, will is will,
the infinite is infinite, nothing is nothing.

—Leo Tolstoy, *A Confession*

[Dark Matter]

The flat black
of the cast iron
pan, the pull of
flame. Not the iron,
its ferromagnetic
birth drawn deep
core of earth;
not the earth
but her elements.
Not the pan,
but the pig iron,
the bituminous ash.
Not the ingot, but
the sand, the mold
to mass; not the load
but the scour, the meld
the eutectic; not
the molten, but the alloy
the liquid tug of mass
to mass; not the cast
but the pan, the gray
tuned to black
patina of lipids
—fat of animal,
of olive, of living
accumulation
of use. Not the
flame, but the
jet, not the jet
but the burning.
Not the flame

but the light;
the wavelength
blued, of red.
Not the spike
but the interval.
What's between,
what's missing;
to be there and
not there; to be
Oakland; to be
and not to be.
The evidence,
the gravitational
lens, the curvature;
postulated, hypothetical
question, rotational
speed of galaxies,
anisotropic apostrophe,
signed and signified.
A hunch, a heft:
a cast iron pan
curing on the stove,
a mundane matter,
dark and certain.

Blind Contours: Night Sky

|* * *| № 3

Since the stereo's playing vintage arrangements, synthetic and pervasive
as microchips, tonight may as well be rushing by
like the city's sodium lights—an amber countdown elapsing its sequence
past the cranked-open sunroof. Your faithfully
falling apart Volkswagen ferries you out past the light-pollution border
to the clarity of ocean air and dark
heavens: the brittle riddle that's annoyed you to steering until the
only road left dead-ends into dirt,
the scruff of rock-brush, black and rolling surf. And now at least
the frame stands still against the sky
and the music's turned kind and melancholic as an old scar—a music
that suits your self-indulgent brood.
Because what haunts your mood isn't as beautiful or false as a girl on a dance
floor where other lights beckon the
unsteady question that troubles your restlessness. You'd curse the stars
if you had the courage, curse the crude
body that propels you through the firmament. And now, because you've
no answer, only more corpulent questions, Vulpecula
foxes herself carefully into the center of your cosmos as the sunroof frames
stars into a simple pattern of coy vixen,
a trickster, a trixie full of guile in the dumb beyond, her slow stumble clarifies
what's left to you—bequeathed as breath.
Take inventory. Breathe and keep doing so.

|* * * *| № 4 [Fata Morgana]

The night is sleep-deprived whilst the Greyhound lists toward dawn.
Landscape falters out the window: you're aching homeward, frazzled

as the fields of Joshua trees stamped against the troubled half-dark.
You can't trust your senses when they reveal the skyline of a distant city

that gleams its broken oath in art-deco arcs & limestone façades, temples of chrome
burnt white, shadow of the dome of pleasure, a prophecy of towers built

from nuclear steam, seams, & edges—ledges of the streamlined Lost Horizon;
Carbide & Carbon, Coit Tower, a Chrysler spire, Boards of Trade, pearl studio

of the imagination; Moderne & rippled radiators anchored in the obsolescence.
City of the aborted future, shroud of parallax. Then a shifting of winds, of gears

grumbling through transmission, a tuning light as the bus angles away from sunrise.
The refraction of glass refocuses form against sky & the phantom polis evaporates

at the edge of night. Less than hallucination, more than semiotic ghost. What's
lost is nothing as tangible as your uncomforting seat, or the stranger slumped against

your shoulder, the orange rind of the fruit she shared with you still perfuming
the sour aisle. A gibbous moon sets toward the Pacific through streaks

of cirrus clouds that superimpose gentle cetacean, streamlined fluke & dorsal,
the moon, her half-closed eye. Your mind seeks pattern, seeks symbol

where none exists in the miles of highway vigil. The bus drifts along postwar
asphalt, plunging further into a continuum you recognize as your own.

SciFi-ku

Eve of chilled stars stuns
the night dark blue. Gravity
holds my place, twirling.

⁕

The rings of Saturn
shimmer, it is said, like white
sand and shells, the shore.

⁕

Venus, Jupiter
dance like forlorn lovers,
each bright birl, pining.

⁕

Asteroids are hurt-
ling in their field. Unlucky
leftovers, poor rocks.

⁕

Telescopic eyes
and such enormity. So
little light squeaks through!

⁕

Robots venture where
we can't. Do servos whir where
there is no sound?

⁕

Earthrise: now we see
how we are seen—enviable,
blue world. So small.

⁕

When stars explode they
color clouds that look like crabs
—even if they don't.

⁕

Starship Enterprise,
its continuing mission
so boldly going.

⁕

Beam me up, Scotty.
Damn it, Jim! I'm a doctor!
Live long and prosper.

⁕

Some neutron stars pulse
accurately as atom-
ic clocks—a heartbeat.

☀

Gauzy ribbon, our
own galaxy, spilled milk sky
—we are but an arm.

☀

We should be a space-
faring people, if only
to leave and come back.

Dispatch

Draw near, good ghost,
  extend your hands
slow as stars
  —secret, vast—
give said dance
  when the present
tense in me
  is a dark sky,
when the oceans
  fall from our shoulders
like horizons.
  This is a dream, this
is a car parked
  in the middle
of the night, this,
  this is the song:

and the sky
  is hazy shade
of winter. Good ghost,
  are we still
on the hood of that wreck?
  Denied our face,
our diffuse grace,
  the sun, its glare.
There, in desert air;
  or here, on a specific
shore; or now, in the
  prophetic city
where morning
  breaks upon the lake,

upon the glass
  upon the stone and brick
of this song. Dear ghost,
  begin your dance.

Grief at the Movies Scrawled in the Dark, Rebooted

When Spock died, I cried—
My friend had not yet died, no, wait
. . . When Kirk died. I lied.

Second Dispatch

Snow falls in the prophetic city   while
I count blessings in broken pentameter.
For thirty years I've held a shallow breath,
lone struggle against my slow and minor
drowning. How I came to be a free man:
walking with arms full of groceries while
my wife delights in the streetlights' sudden
dance of apostrophes—all those years ago,
my absence could not save us. Tonight,
Thomas, I'll dream the weight of our souls
is enough to tip the scales in our favor.
Is this life of burdened bookshelves, sleeping
cats, this pen, this wife, somehow your wish for me?
This city, this snow, our ransomed future tense?

Thirty-Six Weeks

We joke that you're a Plath poem, *ponderous.*
But the truth is, I'm numb with expectation
—these many months rumbling like delivery
trucks. The sidewalks iced, the snow dun,
though the sun casts an even winter-
bright, blue as eyes. What we don't know
is everything, what we can't know is when.

One night soon, you'll wake me and I'll
ferry you through the abandoned streets
to the sterile rooms where waiting is called
labor, where labor is active, where we'll
know with birth's violent certainty
that this happens, has happened, will happen.
To measure, finally, how we've arrived.

Untitled with Teeth Brushed

Open your eyes long enough
it distorts your vision. Pupils contract
into doorway light—that sliver
along the carpet's edge. And let's say
you're remembering Stevens and something
about images making themselves

apparent. And now you're thinking of parents,
or rather, parent—the one made of light:
mother still leaves on the hallway fixture
until she turns herself in; that light casts
in the doorway just-so. And now you're thinking
Stevens couldn't have meant to confuse things so—with words.

It's just light from another room, after all.
Just a bright swath of rug. You left it burning,
remember? Went to brush your teeth. Now,
turn yourself in, shush the light, pass your tongue
across the pearls in your mouth, breath newly minted.
Cross the room, draw the curtains, that between your fingers

remind you of all curtains, those dresses pulled
against the night. Surely this is the more accurate
image, more lasting metaphor—curtains: dress. Hello,
Scarlett O'Hara. She's nothing but a figment,
nothing but movement of thought against light.

Poem Missing My Mother

Weary, I bury
my head
in my folded
arms. Along
my skin,
a smell, sudden
and unmistakable:
tortilla de harina,
jábon y manteca,
aspirin and lilac . . .

The plancha singed
dough is the trail of
moles marching,
matching up
each of my arms.
My vision
is a yellow
kitchen where
I was made
entire.

My Father, Headed East

You've driven this route before. This arid
stretch between ensconced valley floors. Last time
I saw you off: headed east and alone,
May's heavy drone. Me: newly married.
And you: forty pounds heavier—the crime
of fat-and-happy. The horizon shone
and shimmered. When I was a boy, you
explained *heat* and *asphalt*, how they dance
with our eyes at the length of our vision.
You're alone and driving, old dog unrestrained,
arm out the window burning bronze, the trance
of dividing lines and the sun's far off fusion.
    Leaving the land you could never pronounce,
    The drawl and hush you cannot renounce.

Self-Portrait, Hand Tinted

That black-and-white fault,
that candid self-narrative
of sidewalk, winter sun,
dark suit buttons canted
in the faith of forward motion.
Shirt collar thrown open
across lapels. Face, a bas-relief.
Parking meters, palm trees
marking off the vanishing
point just over our pedestrian's
left shoulder. How even there
it's background noise, fog
full of aperture, gray and gray
tree. But a point to begin, brush
green with Easter—something
our pedestrian left behind
that unravels him
in his hurry up the street.

Cuaresma

Restos Mortales

And so I begin to scribble penance.
I'm too careful with my soul not to know
its tarnish has made itself apparent—
a momentary lapse of attention
something grumbled, blasphemous, a gnashing
of teeth. What is it that's written of wrath?
Raise your voice to a slight, feel your fingers
kink to fists. Rage, like an old memory
of rage—like sixteen in a broken town.
Bile and adrenaline rise in your throat,
you're a cornered alley cat: big and black
and bent on living, all piss and instinct.
And for this you think you must repent.

Viernes Santo

Because I would not flinch or turn my face
from what I've witnessed; because I've never
managed to rise from my ashen bed,
I turn westward and confuse grace
with the sun at afternoon's angle—weather
fair, the air sweeps away what I've not said
what I have, and have yet to set
in motion. Why is it blue skies persist
at this solemn hour of the year's regret?
How is it, that even now, my soul resists
those calling winds, that even song of spring?
I am a fool who's blessed with doubt.
Confessed and open, the cemented grout
of this heart, ruined and ready to sing.

Pascua

And like this the sun catches through
the blind-drawn windows, the trees' burgeoning
buds cast true shadow: You realize winter's
greatcoat no longer wears against your
soul's seams. There are omens you should
believe in—the thick almanac of argument—
there are witnesses, here in this room:
The cats sprawled at the carpet's edge where
morning rise still reaches. And you, my love,
wrestle with the overstuffed Sunday edition
I pilfered from the growing pile on the
stoop. These are blessings. And with blessings,
gratitude's obligation: A pen and ink,
a note, simplistically honest, *Thank you.*

Passion Play

Passion, from the Latin—*patior.*
Patior, which is to suffer, which is to endure.
Once again, with feeling. *Passion*
from the Middle French, the suffering
of a martyr—see also Auden: about which
he was never wrong, my Old Master.

Passion, and its etymon: *pass,* to find
conveyance through—a course, a route,
a way in or out of, as in this too will,
which is to endure. See also Tennyson:
"to strive, to seek, to find, and not to yield;"
see also, "let's get the band back together."

At the end of the tenth century: *Passion*,
the suffering of Jesus, see also garden,
a place called Gethsemane, see Matthew 26:38;
see Mark 14:34: "The sorrow in my heart
is so great that it almost crushes me."
(etymon: station—"stay here and keep watch")

—observe yours truly, cassocked and surpliced
bearing a cross from station to station of Christ's
passion: condemnation, crossed, first fall, dear Mother,
Simon's succor, Veronica's kindness, second fall,
O daughters of Jerusalem, third fall, stripped, crucifixion,
ex(s)piration, deposition, entombment.

See yours truly filled with compassion—to suffer with,
to endure companionably—"You must not be afraid."
See also Dr. Donne: "break, blow, burn and make

me new." Please reference the Buddha's Four Sights,
that is to say, foresight, which is witness, which are
visions, and revisions, which is portent, and here is

no great matter: "To Carthage then I came // burning
burning burning burning"—*Passion*, the innate, that
which resides, originating within a matrix, inborn.
Can you dance? Well let's do it! [insert breakdown № 1
o-ah, o-ah, o-o-ah, o-o-o-o-ah]. Popular contrivance
insists you dance, insists you dance like you fuck.

Passion, As a count noun: any strong, controlling,
or overpowering emotion, as desire, hate, fear, etc.;
intense feeling or impulse. Also *personified*.
A literary composition or passage of marked deep,
marked strong emotion; a passionate speech or outburst.
Obs. Please see: Ingraci, H., Professor; Ulrich, J., Emeritus.

Impassion, to fill or inflame with passion—thus to cause
to suffer, thus to make to feel intensely, therefore to pass on,
to give station. Which is to say teach, to teach, to show
to make known, to let one know the cost or penalty; inform,
instruct, educate, school. To forge with anvil and hammer.
See also: "in what furnace was thy brain?" reference fig. A

[insert illuminated manuscript]. Please defer to the autodidact.
Be wary, be warned, forearmed and forthright. *Passion* is not
the absence of reason, yet reason may be passionless. Passion
is not the root of all evil, yet "the worst are filled with passionate
intensity." Passion is not kind, though kin to cruel—it is a mouth,
which is to say that which moves to make its meaning,

meaning the body, the sensual, and pleasures thereof; also
madness, derangement of the mind. See Lowell, "my mind's
not right . . . I myself am hell . . . moonstruck eyes' red fire."
See also: Sexton, Plath, Berryman, et. al. Passion must not
be confused for love, though it is a necessary mistake.
Passion, the pull of body to body, the gravity of desire;

which is to say "careless eyes, lips, and hands;" "believe
in the flesh and its appetites," that, "vegetable love
should grow," though "say no more about 'entwined' . . . beg
'security' to bolt the door," "Full nakedness! All joys are due
to thee, / as souls unbodied, bodies unclothed must be, /
to taste whole joys." Now know that "blood approves, / and kisses

are a better fate / than wisdom." "The Heart asks Pleasure—first—
/ And then—Excuse from pain." *Passion* only ever itself, *patior.*

Un Miércoles en Febrero

The bare elm twisted, light snow stuttering.
What spring promises seems only cruel rumor.

The boy asked me what happened to my forehead.
These ashes, I explain, remind me that

I believe something, but can't recall why
that's so anymore—or why Fridays leave me

hollow. I pretend I'm the peddler of hats
in the boy's storybook, and I've no money

for lunch. I pretend it still means something
to deny the flesh. The boy tells me he likes

my ashes, and asks will I share them?
I press my forehead to his. Faith is doubt,

hijo mío, remember this: we are dust, we are
stars—we are what happened and what is next.

Middle March

You brute.
You too?

Belligerent
sky. Groundhogs

join the rank
road kill.

Jesus. Is this
what you meant by

"Go into your
room and close

the door?"
I cannot parse

the gravel
from the air.

Guesswork Ending in a Levis Fragment

Last picture of you, friend, sealed away
in a surgical gown, a hospital-
white bracelet, your wrist, last wave, that astray
visage—flash-doubled, paradoxical
rainbow refracted against the plastic
wall that failed to keep you safe.
It was medicine's final, most drastic
route. Hematopoietic swap, bone-chafe . . .

And then what? And then what? And then, what
seemed like a long time passed, then curtailed.
Had you guessed by then the magnetic field
is all that is left between us? Please stop,
please. O, this present tense, this wretched skin.
We are something always to be sketched in.

Interruption in *One Hundred Years of Solitude*

. . . An off-kilter sound makes
me look up from Macondo's
paper streets: plosive—a tackle

of stones; piñata cracking open
spilling sweet insides onto concrete.
I know by how abruptly the train slows

that the engineer saw the flash of a face
fall under his tracks; that I had seen
something blue and tumbling out my window.

Someone dumbstruck behind Bay Meadows,
wandering through the haze of horse sweat
and losing numbers: lost rent, squandered

car payment, gambled away groceries
Someone wondering how to two-step
out of his country song—*show place win.*

And I'm clumsy with this stack of postcards
I've meant to send for days—stamped,
addressed, still no *wish you were here.*

The train murmurs and sighs in the mizzle.
The body crumpled a few cars back.
Passengers line up to exit front coach,

walk on to the Hillsdale stop. I stay seated.
Mi mente entre Márquez y la página, soñando;
somniferous sky: I mark the dead bettor

board the train—blue suit, worn and rumpled,
half-Windsor askew, his soul knocked forward
into one hundred minutes from now. And he

falls in line because lines are what
he expects. But when he exits the train
he is confounded. So he presents

himself again to the locomotive's
prow, where he had angled his body
against momentum and steel. Fixes

himself between rails—north and south—where
he embraces his penance: opposing each
oncoming, dispassionate eye. And for months,

trains preoccupied with commuters pass through him
like steam. And each of us feels, for a moment,
something lost: keys, earring, pocketbook, scarf,

billfold, transfer. And only when we finger
an earlobe, make those pocket assurances
do we sense the relief not ours to keep.

Barrio Brisbane Bears Witness

The sidewalk: some neighborhood kids have angled
wide board against cinder block
to ramp up their rollerblades,
and have begun to record the breadth
of their bravery with red, white, green
chalk slashes. Two boys and a girl.

She outjumps her counterparts each time
and they grudgingly lay her green stripe
down past their own and come faster
to the ramp each time—thrill
of gravity defied for however many
seconds: the muscle-clench and wince

of pleasure. They can see in her brown eyes
that she won't decide if she will let
either of them win. They're eleven,
maybe twelve and before the summer
is out she will kiss both these boys.
And how they've begun to admire

her longer, more graceful leaps of faith
in her own brown body. How they look like
they'd never look away as she shakes out
black hair from under her helmet.
How they've suddenly fathomed a want
deeper than any wrapped birthday.

And they see it in each other. And hate
each other for it. And like this, they learn
to conspire. And while they lie in their

beds in houses next door to one another,
they both rise in the unhappy dark,
ripe with orange blossom and gaze across

the street—confused and never before so alone.
Alejandra, Alejandra, each time sweeter
and less forgiven across their lips.
And she skates through their sundried
dreams, *Alejandra, Alejandra*.
And they know vacation will come

for them both, and they are more aware
than ever of those delineated days
—June, July. Joe knows Tony
will leave for a week south to visit
his sunny grandmother. Tony knows
Joe has to go to Silver City as soon

as he returns. And like this,
they become sullen, absorbed in the
delirious glue of model cars, the binary
graphics that entangle their hours—*Alejandra, Alejandra*.
While Tony is away, Joe kisses
Alejandra in the dusk, popsicles melting

in their hands, the sidewalk spotted sticky
and skates still on their feet. Tony brings
Alejandra back a present: Shamu snow globe.
Tony kisses Alejandra beside the pond in the park
while koi look on, murmuring their algae secrets.
Then Alejandra returns to Arizona

after summering with her abuelos. And the boys sit together
on the silent steps of Hilltop Market
watching the last days of August sink
in the miserable sky. *Cherry Popsicle.*
Blazing fish. Alejandra, Alejandra,
abject in their mouths.

The Nostalgic Mode

Sometimes the world seems twenty years ago & wearing a new
pair of shoes—your red brocade dress & the price-tags tucked
in, your stockings, seamed. What were we then but each
other's mouths? Or again hours before, watching you
ready yourself in glass, the brush crushed with stain
dark as cherries across your lips. What we mistook
as desire base as bed sheets blossoming in the dark turned
to something sacred. What I knew then is that I loved
your mouth on mine—the turns of pink parting your pearled
skin. And that, love, is still true. Even as the baby calls in the night.
Even as the old record skips & pops, the stylus electric
as nerves—the song familiar as a cat, a cat in a dream
of a cat curled against the backs of your legs. I woke then
& stayed that way, complete as I am now, which is also true.

The Romantic Mode Overheard

Since the sky's a bad dream—all mist and low ceilings—what started out
as an idea of eggs, slumped into the empty booth of a crowded Belmont diner:
the smoking section, sandwiched between *too-young-to-know-better*
and *the-constant-mistake*. How to romanticize this vinyl and Formica

that's been so thoroughly commodified? Waif and waitress, the scattered
Mohawks of punk's last stand, brokedown drag queens, over-caffeinated
undergrads all spelling their conversations out across fries, pies, the obligatory
steaming cup: those histories of philosophy, those faulted yearnings,

pledges of fidelity, privilege of skin and ignorance. Youth is syndicated,
is on five nights a week. Please, stop talking past each other. Love's
a broken record, kids. Love's a lucky break—a face you know.
Your ten thousand hearts will break tonight, and your hearts

are well rehearsed: practiced all month dropping glasses, vases,
bottles of blood-red wine, half empty. *I wish it could have been different.*
I thought we were so true, you know? Eyes so green they wrecked me.
Take it outside. The mercury is steady, the mist is wished for and easily forgets.

Manny's Luck Runs Out: A Parlor Trick

So there I am, sittin' at the table,
I musta had three hundred bucks
in front of me. So I decide now's
the time to bet big, ya know.

I musta had three hundred bucks,
and the dealer's been good to me.
So it's the time to bet big, ya know.
I got the feelin' that my cards are comin'.

And the dealer, he's been good to me,
so I bet a silver dollar on his end—
I got the feelin' that my cards are comin',
see—so I put up a straight hundred,

and a silver dollar on the dealer's end.
Out come the bullets, two to my right,
and I put up that straight hundred
and I'm thinkin', here it comes.

Out come the bullets, two to my right,
but he hit me with a heavy seven.
That seven made my gut tighten up,
and I'm thinkin' here it comes.

But he hits me with another heavy seven,
and he's showin' a six, so I'm thinkin'
right, even though that seven made my gut tighten up,
I gotta split these bastards, right.

’Cause he’s only showin’ a six. And so I’m thinkin’.
But that’s another hundred on the table,
’cause I gotta split these bastards up, right.
So I put up another hundred,

but that’s another hundred on the table.
The dealer, he splits ’em for me, then.
So I put up another hundred, and he
pops my first seven with another seven!

The dealer, he splits ’em for me again,
so that’s all three hundred on the table.
He popped my first seven with another seven!
And I’m pissed ’cause that woulda hit twenty-one.

So that’s all three hundred on the table,
my whole fuckin’ wad, and I’m startin’ to sweat it,
and I’m still pissed, ’cause I woulda hit twenty-one.
So out they come, an Ace a Queen and a Jack,

and my whole fuckin’ wad is out there, and I’m sweatin’,
two seventeens and a soft eight against his six.
They came straight out, an Ace a Queen and a Jack.
So, I’m thinkin’ I’m gonna double my wad, right?

Two seventeens and a soft eight against his six,
I got all three hundred on the fuckin’ table,
and I’m thinkin’ I’m gonna double my wad.
Son of a bitch turns a Queen and a five!

I got all three hundred on the fuckin' table,
my whole fuckin' game gone in one hand.
Son of a bitch turns a Queen and a five!
I couldn't fuckin' believe it.

My whole game gone in one hand. And the
waitress finally shows with a whiskey,
I still couldn't believe it. But
there I am, sitting at the table.

Final Epistle to My Grad-School Self

Hey Menso,

Quit thinking you're special. No eres. Quit thinking that you are your oppressor, quit thinking you don't belong amidst them. Wear their skin like Xipe Totec—mingle like hands in air, follow the scent of blood to the source, keep your blade as sharp as your words. Just because they let you sit at the table and talk, don't think they take you as seriously as they take themselves. Learn how to stand up for yourself on each desert ridge and take that landscape with you in that place you call *home*; if you always make this landscape interior, you will never feel displaced in cities of glass and stone, never lose your way in the foreign forests for long, never confuse the repeated white faces for kin, for kind. Remember when you were in kindergarten, how then the kids wouldn't let you in their playground because you are Mexican and Catholic—both somehow less offensive than how much you look like them. Know that the stars in the sky are the same as they ever were. Remember how to use a compass. Remember how to construct a sentence. Always serve your sentence completely. Just because you're silent, doesn't mean you're not a wreck waiting for metal. Remember your name, remember it is the one your mother gave you to protect you against the bluest eyes. Even as you master the tongue, you master another. Sometimes they let you in the club because you're handsome. Sometimes because you're smart. Sometimes because you pronounce so beautifully into their ears those rolled erres. Remember your passport. Speak the truth always, even if it leads to your death. You will sometimes wonder how you made your way past their company. You are always both, and neither. La duda no dura. El hombre prevenido vale por dos.

$N = R^{*} \text{ x } f_p \text{ x } n_e \text{ x } f_\ell \text{ x } f_i \text{ x } f_c \text{ x } L : \text{" } \forall \text{ "}$

{The Drake Equation Ending in Fermi's Paradox}

Where R^{*} is the rate of our elliptic tour while galactic births of dust to disc to firing of far-off fusions ignite to stars—each violent, each ordinary—multiplied by the fraction of suns that tune remainders to spheres that themselves accord to heliocentric systems;

and of these planets multiply again the aggregate division to divine those worlds which may support the biological insistence of cellular organization, and of those worlds once more the poor portion where apposite models flourish, blossom, reproduce through what means best suit their fit and finish, so that, as here on earth, what arises profluates into its specialized breath.

Until this gradual divergence plateaus, fixates, adapts entirely, knows finally it lives until it dies, knows finally loss and lack, turns to companion for solace, utters a sound that means, and companion utters back.

And now there is narrative, which is to say impetus. (This is to acknowledge that the fault of ideas is that they are our own, an anthropic coincidence). Language can hold thought only long enough to reason—to distill experience to foresight.

So clans arise, so tribes,
villages and hamlets, craft and trade and avarice. So weapons are forged, so plows and scythes.
So conquerors are made and slaves. So cities are built and sacked, rebuilt and burned. So covenants are sealed, violated; so resources

consumed and spoiled, so feuds, so wars
so the dead are disposed, so hate, so grudges, so greater weapons—range and subterfuge.
So politic, so empire, so the stratified society.

Then industry, then economics, then theories of inconstant peace. And of these worlds, and of these peoples, the fractions that emerge from strife to standoff to suspicion; then machines, then monitor and monitored. So the code, so the beam.

And so the masses are assuaged, so facsimiles are made and paid. The pixilated, the digitized. Poor stewards of a blue and envious world.

This endless babble, this civilized technology, this cosmic static.

Fulano's Last Law of Memento

Mind the blank page tonight—threatening
its possibility of fourteen lines, a promised
disappointment, succinct as a kiss: broken words
singing like stars in someone else's sky.

Chaos works through its agenda of dust. The sure
potential of a pencil, yellow paint and core
of ceramic carbon—graphite wearing itself
into some deliberate dust. *Remember that*

you are dust, and to dust you shall return,
your forehead marked with the bruise
of faith. Lent is also past tense, the ruined
participle; and when you forget

all I've borrowed or how much, I'll return
to you keys and a basketball, ball-point pens,
every dollar, every ounce of good fortune
—kind words like *whirlwind* and *star.*

Stars are made of dust and gravity: whirlwinds
of pressure that ignite into complicated equations
set down in pencil; pencils, as mentioned,
should be wielded like hammers high upon

a roof in disrepair, elegant as nails and sure
as force. It takes force to drive nails flush,
force to press the delicate lead into elegant
numbers on a page that describe exactly

some far off heavenly hypothesis. Every hypothesis
waits like a good child for some bright reward.

Notes

The William Carlos Williams epigraph for section 1 is from the poem "El Hombre," from his early collection *Al Que Quiere!* (Four Seas Company, 1917).

Blind Contours: Night Sky № 1, "a quintessence of dust," from *Hamlet* (II, ii) by Wm. Shakespeare.

Purgatory Adjacent: A Dreamscape, is for Bayo Olayinka Ojikutu.

A Science Fiction is inspired by several theories that hypothesize what might happen should a human being be pulled into a black hole and is for Ursula K. LeGuin.

The Li-Young Lee epigraph for section 2 is from his poem, "Station," from his book *Behind My Eyes* (W. W. Norton & Company, 2008).

The Hubble Meditations are based on deep space images taken by land-based telescopes and the Hubble Space Telescope and are indebted to the diligent work of the National Aeronautics and Space Administration and the Space Telescope Science Institute. The images these poems are based on are readily available on the internet.

Ojo de Dios, "fluent in the idiom of blue," from James Merrill's poem "The Blue Eye," *Selected Poems* (Knopf, 1993). This poem is based on the image of the Helix Nebula, more commonly known as the Eye of God.

Deep Field Image, "the finale of seem," from Wallace Stevens' poem "The Emperor of Ice Cream," *The Palm at the End of the Mind: Selected Poems and a Play* (Vintage, 1990).

The Leo Tolstoy epigraph for section 3 is from *A Confession and Other Religious Writings* (Penguin Classics, 1988).

Blind Contours: Night Sky № 4 borrows ideas from William Gibson's short story "The Gernsback Continuum," *Burning Chrome* (Ace, rev. ed. 1986). The phrase "the shadow of the dome of pleasure" from Samuel Taylor Coleridge "Kubla Khan."

Cuaresma is for Richard Jones.

Passion Play was originally composed, in a different version, for the "Passionate Professors Lecture" given to the English Honors Society at DePaul University in 2010. All poetic quotations and borrowed definitional language come from *The Norton Anthology of Poetry*, 5th ed. and the *Oxford English Dictionary* online, respectively.

About the Author

Photo credit: Joshua Brown

Carl Marcum is a Chicano poet from Tucson, Arizona. He is the author of the collection *Cue Lazarus*, and his poems have appeared in the anthologies *The Wind Shifts: New Latino Poetry* and *Latinx Rising: An Anthology of Latinx Science Fiction & Fantasy*. He received his MFA from the University of Arizona and was a Wallace Stegner Fellow at Stanford University. Marcum has been awarded fellowships from the National Endowment for the Arts, the Illinois Arts Council, and the Taos Writers Conference. He served as a Canto Mundo Fellow from 2011–2015. Marcum taught for many years at DePaul University in Chicago and now lives in Pittsburgh, Pennsylvania, where he is the managing director of a small engineering and environmental consulting firm in the Marcellus Shale.